D1537808

RENEWALS: 691-4574
DATE DUE

MAP

M

LIBRARY
The University of Texas
At San Antonio

EASY READING INFORMATION SERIES

GLASS

Written by O. B. Gregory
Illustrated by Denis Wrigley

© 1981 Rourke Publications
1975 O. B. Gregory

Library of Congress Cataloging in Publication Data

Gregory, O. B. (Olive Barnes), 1940-
  Glass.

  (Easy reading information series)
  Summary: Describes how glass is made by
heating sand with other materials in a furnace
and molded, blown, or rolled into bottles,
windows, and other things. Includes questions
and vocabulary.   I. Glass—Juvenile literature.
[1. Glass]   I. Wrigley, Denis, ill.   II. Title.
III. Series.
TP857.3.G73   666'.1   81-11891
ISBN 0-86625-163-4   AACR2

ROURKE PUBLICATIONS, INC.
Windermere, Fla. 32786

GLASS

Glass is very useful to us.

We use it in many ways.

We use it to make windows.

We use it to make bottles.

We use it to make glasses.

We use it to make jars.

We use it to make many other things.

Glass is made from sand.

Other things are mixed with the sand.

Broken glass is also added
and mixed with the sand.

Everything is now ready for the furnace.

A furnace is like a big oven and it
is very hot indeed.

A furnace is kept burning day and night
for two or three years.

The sand and other things
     are put into the furnace.

All these things mix together
     and become melted glass.

The melted glass is hot and sticky.

Next, it is cooled a little.

If the glass is being made into bottles
     it runs along a channel.

At the end of the channel
     it drops through a hole.

As it drops, enough is cut off
to make a glass or bottle.

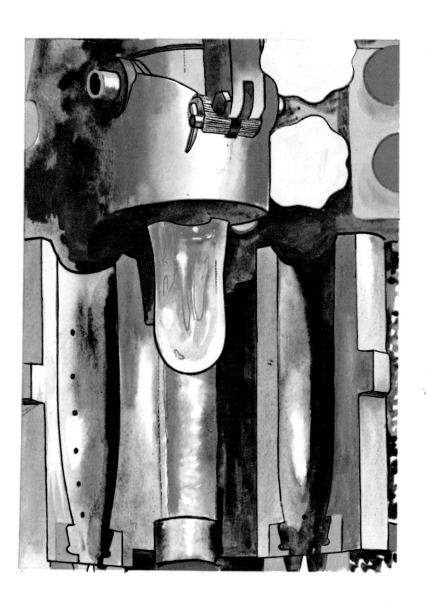

The lump of sticky, melted glass
drops into a mold.

The mold is shaped like a bottle
which has been placed
upside down.

The glass drops into the mold
and is pressed into shape.

At first, it is pressed into a shape
something like a bottle.

Then it is put into another mold.

Hot air is blown inside
to make the finished shape.

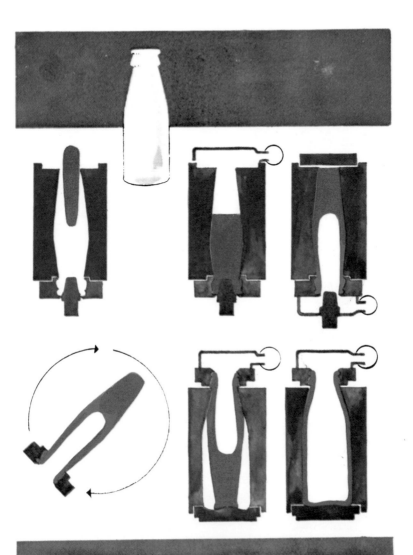

The bottles must now be cooled.

This must be done slowly
or the bottles would break.

The bottles go on a moving belt
through a long oven.

In the oven they are heated again
so as to make them strong.

Then they are cooled slowly.

As the bottles leave the oven
a man looks at them carefully.

He does this to see that
the bottles are well made.

Most bottles are made by machine.

But a few kinds of glass
        are made by blowing.

A man gets a ball of melted glass
        on the end of an iron tube.

He blows down the tube
        and shapes the glass into a ball.

This can then be blown
        into whatever shape is wanted.

Sometimes, machines are used.

Part of a glass is made by blowing
        and part is made by machine.

Sheets of glass for windows
are drawn from tanks
of melted glass.

First of all, an iron bar
is dipped into the glass.

As the bar is pulled up
some melted glass sticks to it.

The glass is passed through rollers
to keep it flat and smooth.

Then it passes through a cooling tower.

As it comes out at the top
the glass is cut into different sizes.

Cars use a special kind of glass.

This is called safety glass.

Safety glass must be very strong.

It is made in this way:

Sheets of glass are heated in furnaces
    until they almost begin to melt.

The glass is then cooled suddenly
    by jets of cold air.

If safety glass is broken
    it breaks into small, blunt pieces.

These do not hurt so much
    as sharp pieces of glass.

Some churches have
   stained glass windows.

Stained glass windows are pictures
   made of many pieces
   of colored glass.

Colored glass is made by adding
   different things to the sand.

The glass is made by blowing.

The man gets a ball of melted glass
   at the end of an iron tube.

He blows down the tube
   and shapes the glass
   into a cylinder.

The cylinder of hot glass is cut open
   and laid out until it is flat.

The glass is cut into small pieces
of different shapes and sizes.

Marks are painted on the glass
to show lines and shadows.

Sometimes writing is painted
on the glass.

The pieces are then put together
like the pieces of a jig-saw puzzle.

The separate pieces of glass
are held together by strips of lead.

The window is made in the workshop
and is then taken to the church.

THINGS TO WRITE

1. Glass is made from _____. (4)

2. Broken _____ is mixed with the sand. (4)

3. A furnace is a big _____. (4)

4. Melted glass runs along a _____. (6)

5. The glass runs along a _____. (6)

6. Then it drops through a _____. (6)

7. It drops into a _____. (8)

8. It is _____ into shape. (8)

9. Hot _____ is blown inside the mold. (8)

10. The bottles must be cooled _____. (10)

11. Most bottles are made by _____. (12)

12. Sheets of glass are drawn from
    _____.   (14)

13. Cars use _____ glass.   (16)

14. Safety glass is cooled _____.   (16)

15. Some churches have _____ glass
    windows.   (18)

16. The glass is made by _____.   (18)

17. The man blows down the _____. (18)

18. He shapes the glass into a
    _____.   (18)

19. The glass is cut into small _____. (20)

20. The pieces are held together
    by strips of _____.   (20)

VOCABULARY

FURNACE — a structure which can give off a great deal of heat. You probably have a furnace to heat your home.

CHANNEL — a rut or groove into which water or other liquids can run. A river could be considered a large channel.

MOLD — a hollow form into which something liquid is poured. The liquid hardens and is removed and it has the same shape as the mold.

JET — a stream of water or other liquid which is moving very forcefully.

CYLINDER — a round shape which is hollow in the middle and open at the ends.

JIG-SAW PUZZLE — a puzzle which has irregularly shaped pieces which fit together to make a picture.